First in the Family

ADVICE ABOUT COLLEGE FROM FIRST-GENERATION STUDENTS

Your High School Years

BY KATHLEEN CUSHMAN

NEXT GENERATION PRESS

Providence, Rhode Island

Next Generation Press
P.O. Box 603252
Providence, RI 02906
www.nextgenerationpress.org

ISBN 0-9762706-3-3

For additional copies in quantities of ten or more,
please contact Next Generation Press at
info@nextgenerationpress.org.

Book design by Sandra Delany.

10 9 8 7 6 5 4 3 2 1

Acknowledgments

Support for this book came from Lumina Foundation for Education. The opinions expressed here are those of the authors and do not necessarily represent official policies or positions of Lumina Foundation for Education.

Abe Louise Young and Montana Miller conducted some of the student interviews from which this book emerged. They also played a crucial role in shaping its content and focus, as did Barbara Cervone and Celia Bohannon. Additional thanks to Montana Miller for her interviewing advice and flawless transcriptions, and to Abe Louise Young for her superb final editing of the manuscript.

Next Generation Press owes its greatest thanks to the students whose insights and advice make up the substance of this book. They came to us with the assistance of the following people and organizations: Mamta Motwani Accapadi at the University of Texas in Austin; Patty Chong-Delon at City College of San Francisco; Pete Coser at Oklahoma State University; Chris Douse at Indiana University–Purdue University Fort Wayne; John Hilley and Anderson Williams at Community IMPACT in Nashville; Virginia Jane Rosser at Bowling Green State University in Ohio; Darrick Smith at Oakland Technical Arts High School; and Irene Sterling at the Paterson Education Fund.

Contents

Introduction

*T*his booklet might be one of your first steps in thinking about college, or you might have been thinking about it already for some time. Unlike other advice books on getting to college, this one will not hand you a recipe filled with instructions. Instead, as you read it you should keep in mind the "three C's" of your college journey:

Conversation, Connections, and *Confidence.*

First, this book is a *conversation* with students who, like you, are the first in their family to go on to college. Most of them have just finished their second year in college, and they are going on for more. They remember very well what it was like to be in high school, aiming for college without relatives to guide them. As you read their stories, perhaps you can think of them as older cousins, sitting in a comfortable place with you and passing along what they have learned. The students who helped write this book hope that their conversation will open up new possibilities to you, as you think about your own future.

Second, the *connections* you make between these students' stories and your own life will help you on your way to college. You might be having some of the very same experiences they did, or your family background might have something in common with theirs. As you read, connect what they did with what you might also do, some day soon. Make your own list of ideas, try them out, and see where they take you.

Finally, these students hope that their stories and words will give you *confidence* as you work toward your college goal. Each one of them has made it to college and is doing well there, even though no one in their families went before them. If they can do it, so can you!

1

You Are College Material

Believe in your right to college

*H*azel Janssen thinks of herself as an artist. "I love to act," she says, "but I also knit, I sew, I shoot and edit movies." When she found herself crammed into the over-crowded classrooms of a huge Denver high school, she fell behind in her work and lost interest in school. "I need a lot of attention," she says. "If I have questions, I need them answered. And I work better at my own pace." At sixteen, she dropped out and moved in with her boyfriend. She decided not to worry about college. Maybe she didn't even need it, since she wanted to live the artist's life. Her father and mother did not have college degrees, so why should she?

Six months later, Hazel was having second thoughts. College might help her find a job that paid more—or maybe she could learn acting or directing in a college program. But she had another worry. At this point, what college would want her? Was she even "college material"?

All around the country, young people ask themselves that question, especially those whose parents did not go to college. Not all of these students choose to drop out of high school, as Hazel did. They might get their diplomas and then look for work instead of aiming for higher education. They might stick it out in high school, but notice that nobody ever mentions college as an option for them.

You may already be planning your way to college. But if not—if your situation sounds like any of these—you could be asking yourself, "Am I college material?" In the pages that follow, other first-generation students tell how they said yes to that question. They describe how they overcame obstacles and made it to college. These ideas, strategies, and encouragements from those who have accomplished the journey can help you get there, too.

Before you decide not to go to college, picture yourself there.

"A little country and a little ghetto" is how Stephen Torres describes his upbringing. He was raised on seven acres, surrounded by grandparents, aunts, and cousins in a somewhat rural black and Latino neighborhood near Austin, Texas. His father, a barber, did not have much interest in college, but his mother always wished that the pressures of parenthood had not ended her education.

Early in his teens, while watching a University of Texas baseball game on television, Stephen realized there was a university just fifteen minutes from his home. An athlete himself, he began imagining himself there.

》 College was this abstract thing that people talked about, but seeing it on TV, with the same skyline as my city . . . I was like, "Wow, maybe I can attend that university." - STEPHEN

Up until then, he had known that his parents expected him to go on to college. They were always pushing him to do well in school. But from then on, when he thought about college, it was a real place. When he had the choice in his senior year of high school, he chose to apply to the school near home, with the skyline he knew so well.

Out in Oakland, California, Niema Jordan knew that plenty of universities lay within striking distance of the gritty streets of home. But she and her high school friends could not quite picture themselves there, until the teacher of her leadership class took a group to visit the college he had attended himself. Only an hour from her high school, its leafy green campus seemed a world away.

》 Stepping foot on a college campus as a high school student puts you that much closer. You can only go after things that you know about, that's the thing. You go visit a college, and maybe you don't like that college. But you find something there that's interesting, that you could possibly get into. Maybe they have a publication on campus that you thought was really cool. Maybe they have a nice hangout spot. It makes it more tangible, something that you can grasp and build on. It shows you college is attainable. You're not enrolled, but you're here on the campus, which means you can get there, you know what I'm saying? - NIEMA

Across the Bay Bridge from Niema, in San Francisco, Naixing Lei was still struggling to learn the English language. He came from China at the age of sixteen with his parents, who had been farmers there. As a junior in high school, looking for a way to work off stress, he started going with Chinese-speaking classmates to play tennis on the courts of a nearby community college.

》 At that point I did not think about going into college. The only purpose I went to the college for was to play tennis. But actually I made a couple friends. One is a girl and the other one is a boy, and they are Chinese. They go here, they are college students, and they know more English than I did. By taking that chance, you are able to meet people at the college. Then they will serve you as a bridge. – NAIXING

Two years later, Naixing still plays tennis on those community college courts, but now he is studying for his own degree there, and planning to go further after that.

It's not too late for anybody to go to college.

Attending high school in rural Indiana, John Berry did not work very hard at his classes. Almost no one else went to college from his school.

》 I came from a high school where you did the bare minimum. That was basically the expectation. The overwhelming majority of my classmates' parents farmed, so that's what a lot of them went on to do. Most of my friends either went into the military or started their families, worked in restaurants or grocery stores, got factory jobs.

I worked in a factory making door panels for Subarus, and then I moved to the city and worked as the night kitchen manager for a restaurant. When they closed the place, I ended up doing maintenance for a moving company. It just wasn't what I was meant to do. I'm not mechanically inclined at all. I have to think which way to turn a screwdriver to tighten a screw!

I thought, "This is not the job for me," but I had bills to pay. I had two options: I could either go back to school or move back with my family. I always knew in the back of my mind that the only real way I'm ever going to make anything of myself is to go back to school. – JOHN

John was already 25 years old when he applied for college, and he chose a commuter college* (Indiana University–Purdue University Fort Wayne) where the average student is 24 years old. Once enrolled, he kept working at a restaurant job, and took a full course load as well. He plans to go on for a graduate degree, and wants some day to teach history at a university. "College is what you make of it," he says. "You can do anything if you make time for it."

If you aren't already on the college track, you can start over from where you find yourself now.

While Jackie Comminello studied to be a dental hygienist at the Community College of Denver, she also helped her boyfriend reconsider his college plans. She knew that, like her, he needed support to believe he could succeed.

>> I met him in ninth grade, and he wasn't into school. So he ended up getting his GED 'cause he didn't graduate, and then I tried to talk him into going to community college here. He struggled with the same exact things that I did: "What if I'm not up to the level?" or "I don't think I'm smart enough." I'm like, "No, you're smart enough, I know it, I believe in you!" Finally, I went down there and applied with him. He got a scholarship, and he's been going to school ever since. He's so smart and I'm so proud of him. He did the remedial classes first, 'cause he tested at a lower level, so he was working on that for a long time. Now he's working on his last prerequisites to go for a two-year fire sciences program, and then he'll have his associates degree. He keeps getting better and better at school. – JACKIE

Once you start down the road, you can define yourself as "on the way to college."

Aileen Rosario moved with her family to Paterson, New Jersey when she was sixteen. Both of her parents are Dominican immigrants with no English, and they worried about bad influences in the Bronx, where they had been living. They had reasons to worry. Most of Aileen's six siblings

---

* At a commuter college, students attend classes but do not live at the college.

dropped out of high school; three young nephews now live with her and her mother, while her brother serves time in jail.

Aileen dreamed of a career in law, though she had only a vague sense of how to achieve that. Steered into low-level classes at a huge and overcrowded school, she first aimed only to get her high school diploma. She received good grades, Aileen recalled, but her senior-year counselor told her, "Forget about college."

Her luck picked up in twelfth grade, when a business-oriented class helped her find an after-school internship with a community organization. Seeing her strengths, her supervisors there urged her on. "They really pushed me," Aileen said. They helped her research schools and guided her through the process of college visits and application. Two years later, she was still working there—while studying for her associates degree.

Once Aileen chose to define herself in her family as "the one who's going to college," doors opened up for her. Even the obstacles she faced gave her new pride and energy.

>> My identity in my house, 'cause I come from a big family, is "the one that goes to college, the one that's trying to do something for her life." My brother's the one with the three kids who live with us, my other sister's the single mother raising two kids on her own, my other sister's only nineteen with a one-year-old son, and the other one is working in food services, the same job like my mother. Everybody looks at me, they're proud of me. Just to know that somebody is proud of you makes you even reach for more. – AILEEN

The motivation to go to college comes from inside *you*.

>> I had friends but they did not speak a single word about going to college. I realized by myself, by feeling. – NAIXING

Even if your family or friends have no idea how to help you, choosing to aim for college will make a difference in your relationship. People who have more knowledge and resources than you will notice, too, and may want to help.

Eric Polk spent his high school years in East Nashville, Tennessee, at a high school ranked at the bottom of the city's list. Supported by AFDC*,

---

*Aid to Families with Dependent Children, a government program to help low-income families.

he lived with his mother and younger sister in the poorest section of town. His friends on the streets knew of his ambitions, and they steered him away from trouble so he could aim higher. He let people know the future he wanted, and that helped him in the long run.

》 Education was going to be my ticket out of here. The first train that comes to Nashville, I'm getting on it. I won't be defined by a statistic, like "how people who grow up in this area are more likely to turn out." Not me! I won't! - ERIC

Niema's mother worked as a security guard and her stepfather drove a bus; they had other children to care for, so their time and energy ran short. As Niema made her way toward college, she decided to treat that as a positive thing.

》 I didn't have anybody to walk me through the process of getting into college, so I pretty much have that "go-for-it, figure things out on your own" attitude. It prepares you for college. Now that I'm here, I think I have the easiest time picking out classes out of all my friends who go here. - NIEMA

Put yourself in the picture and imagine the satisfaction.

As a student at Wake Forest University, Eric still recalls the thrill of the day his college acceptance letter came.

》 So my mom kind of nonchalantly hands me the envelope and she walks upstairs . . . I was tearing it slowly and looking at it. I didn't even read the whole thing, I just read "Congratulations," and I screamed. My mom turned right around and basically fell down the stairs—we hugged and we cried, and—emotions breakdown—I got in! I mean that was the longest haul of my life! I called everybody in my cell phone book. To hear people's reactions on the line, screaming, "He got in, he got in!" The whole neighborhood: "What? Eric's going to Wake Forest!" Everybody knew that I'd been waiting for this, so it was like, "We knew it, we knew it, he got in!" My friends threw me a party. They were like, "Oh dude, we are going out this weekend." And of course, my teacher Miss Q, I had to call and tell her, and she cried. By morning everybody in school knew about it. They made a huge announcement over the intercom, "Congratulations to Eric Polk, the first Stratford student ever to get accepted to Wake Forest University!" - ERIC

All over the country, students like Eric—and like you—are breaking new ground, holding the title as the first in the family to go to college. The first step to that position is thinking of yourself as college material: believing you are capable, and knowing you deserve the chance.

2

We Can Do Better

Mike Morris played football for his high school team in rural Mississippi. He calls himself "one of those guys who lived and breathed off what their team did." The state college recruited him to play for them, but once he got there he had trouble with academics. "I'm not a person that loves to go to school," he says. He dropped back to junior college to catch up, and he was thinking seriously about taking a job instead.

Still, Mike felt deep loyalty to the beloved aunt who had raised him from the time he was a baby, when his mother was hospitalized with an ongoing illness. He dreamed of making enough money to buy his aunt a house and reward her years of struggle. So when a football recruiter from Brigham Young University offered him a place there, Mike made up his mind to go. A quiet person who guards his privacy, he was lonely so far from home. He found the Utah college a completely foreign setting, from social life to religion, geography, and climate. When a foot injury kept him off the playing field, he had to think hard about whether college was worth the effort.

Many students have the same question Mike did, whether they face it in high school or afterward. In the following pages, they tell about what they decided, and give their reasons why.

A college education can change not just your life, but also the lives of people in your family and community.

As Mike thought about whether he should go to college in faraway Utah or just get a job in rural Mississippi, he looked at the experiences of others in his family.

>> It's been a lot of missed opportunities. In my family, we have a lot of males that just don't do anything; they're real athletic in high school and then just stop. My uncle, who's in a factory now, he dropped out of high school when his mom died. I kind of made up my mind I needed to do something to set the standard, make everyone want to do something. - MIKE

He thought of his aunt working for years in a factory to support him and her daughter.

>> It's kind of hard when you're in college and you look back at her! To this day now, she won't miss a day. She can be sick, but she still goes. I'm in college—most people would say for themselves, trying to build themselves. I'm in college for *them*—to better them, give them a chance. If anything were to happen to me after that, I don't care. But as long as I can get my aunt her first house, her first own land, and help my cousin out with her child, I'm happy. - MIKE

At the University of Texas, close to the Mexican-American neighborhood where he grew up, Stephen began to think of his college experience as a political force affecting the lives of other Latinos as well.

>> In high school, from the down looking up, I would never have expected college to be like this. I saw college as "get this degree, this piece of paper, so you can move on to get a good job and make some money and have a family and do great things with your life." And there's so much more! It's interesting to realize how much power we have as students. We organize and coordinate all the events for the Latino community. We're in charge of making groups united on campus and fostering communication and empowerment among the community. I worked for the City Council this past summer, so people know who I am when I walk into City Hall. It sounds kind of stupid to say, but I feel like I'm important! - STEPHEN

Consider the alternatives you face without a college degree.

Attending a technical high school in Oakland, Niema often heard friends say that they had better things to do with their time than go to college.

>> You have to think about, what does "better with your time" mean? You may say, "Well, I know somebody who makes such and such amount of money," but those people are exceptions to the rule. There's no guarantee that you will be the next exception. Think about where that part-time or full-time job is going to have you in ten years, as opposed to where college is going to have you in ten years. You can find statistics anywhere on the difference between the salaries of a high school graduate and a college graduate.

> I think one of the main things that prevents people from going to college is not being able to see far enough into the future. I think it comes from always having to worry about the here and now. My mom was never worried about how she was going to feed me in ten years. She was worried about how she was going to get food on the table for tonight. — NIEMA

Like Niema's parents, Naixing's mother and father made enormous sacrifices so that their children could get better jobs than they had. When he first came to this country, Naixing says he did not think of college. But as he watched his parents, he changed his mind.

» My parents worked as farmers who grow oranges, as merchants on the street stands selling homegrown vegetables. Later, they worked as waiters in the Chinese food restaurants where the owners often abused and scolded them for unreasonable reasons. One day my mom's thumb got injured when she was chopping a piece of pork on the chopping board. I helped wrap the wound with cotton cloth and her hands look so badly that I could not describe them. Feeling sorry and compassionate, I questioned my mom for the cause. And she gave me one response: "the scar of laborious work."

As I saw my parents work earlier and get home later, I started to feel that I should do better and make a career. For me, a good job—doctor, lawyer, manager, financial consultant—does not require excessive physical effort, but offers higher compensation in a short period of work time. College is a stepping-stone to get a good job, a high-paying job in the future. — NAIXING

Aileen, too, saw how difficult life was for her mother, father, and older sisters and brothers. For her, being a financially independent woman was a powerful goal.

» My mother works in the public school, in the food service department, she's like a lunch lady. With a lot of kids to take care of, it was kind of hard for her. But she's like, "I don't want this for you, I want you to be somebody." She didn't want us to have the struggle she had. I saw how my sisters ended up, and all that they still are going through, with kids, married to somebody older. They weren't happy with their life, and they didn't have anything to show for it. So that got me thinking, I really don't want to have to struggle like this. I don't want to have to pick somebody just for financial reasons. I didn't want to go work at a low-paying, $5.15 an hour, regular job. I wanted something more. – AILEEN

After Hazel dropped out of her unsatisfying high school and went to work while living with her boyfriend, she found the search for a job far worse than she had expected.

》 I got a close-up view of what it's like to be out there in the real world, without a high school diploma, without any college education. Finding a job is murder. You cannot work anywhere for more than seven dollars an hour! I called jobs every day in the paper, and even for a door-to-door job they wouldn't let me earn more! So I figured out early on that if I didn't get any more schooling, this was going to be my life. I would be working maybe three jobs, just to pay for one crappy apartment. And that's not the way I want to live. There are people who do that and work very hard at it, and you know, I have respect for them! Because I couldn't do it. I would collapse in a quivering mass of flesh. – HAZEL

Jackie, the student who helped her boyfriend join her at community college, first got focused on college when she saw the future that faced her friends in one of Denver's poorest high schools.

》 I hung out with a lot of people, but they weren't really into school and that's probably why I ditched at first too. I thought, "Well, I finally found people that are cool with me, so I might as well hang out with them," and that's how I ended up.

After a while I told them, "I have to straighten up," and I was going to class. They started feeling the same way, a little bit. But when I talked to them about going to college, they're like, "Are you serious? Who goes to college here?" Even from the ninth, tenth grade we had a high rate of people dropping out, getting pregnant, or the guys having to drop out too, to take care of their girl. I think they kind of wanted that to happen, because they're so used to that—generation by generation, their parents dropped out of school early. That's what made me dummy up, like, "I need to wake up, I need to get focused on school." – JACKIE

College is a chance to learn about yourself and follow your own ideas.

Hazel dropped out of high school partly because her learning style didn't match its fast-paced schedule of short periods that met every day. When she decided to go back to school, she chose a situation that combined high school with community college classes. That pace suited her much better.

» At my first high school, homework was horrible. Every day, every day, "Here, do this," with very little explanation, and then the teacher would go off to help another student. The class size was huge, just packed to the brim, so you got very little attention from the teacher as an individual. You went by your school ID number, it was almost like that was your name.

I work better if it's at my own pace, which is what I'm doing now. There's still deadlines, but it's easier to get things done. They don't penalize you for not getting your homework done "this day at this time." - HAZEL

When Niema got to college, she also found its flexibility one of the things she liked best. Not only could she choose the subjects she wanted to study, but she could often choose the times she went to class.

» One of my friends, she didn't want to go to college because she thought college was too hard. I was like, "Excuse me? No no no." This is the greatest thing. If I don't want to wake up before eleven o'clock, I don't have to! I get to pick what classes I'm taking and when those classes are. First quarter, my earliest class was eleven o'clock, and three days out of the week I was done by one. It was like all this free time in the world! Yay! Can't do it in high school. Doesn't happen.

In college there's more leeway, and that's something else a lot of people don't know. They go, "Oh, I don't want people telling me what to learn, I'm so sick and tired of people being on my case. And college is going to be too much work." And that's really not the case, you know? I have to take three literature classes, and I don't want to read any more Shakespeare ever again in my life. So, my choice? I took an African Literature class, this quarter I'm going to take an African-American Lit class, and next year I'm going to take Japanese Literature. You have that choice. College gives you options, and there's so many things to learn about that you couldn't find in high school. - NIEMA

Making Your Map

How to find information and set your sights on college

*A*ileen Rosario had all she could do just to survive eleventh grade. Her family had just moved to New Jersey and she had not yet found friends at the huge Paterson high school. Having fallen behind the year before, she had to take extra courses if she was going to graduate with her class. Her older sister, always her closest companion, had just quit school and was no longer there to support her.

To make things worse, Aileen couldn't seem to get the attention of the school guidance office. She worked hard and got on the honor roll, but no one ever talked about going to college. She didn't know that she should take the SAT before applying, let alone how to sign up for it.

Although Aileen's parents liked the idea of her attending college, they didn't have much idea about what it would involve. "I couldn't talk to anybody in my house, because nobody knew," she says. "They were just like, 'Oh, whatever college you go to it doesn't matter. You could go to a trade school if you want.'"

By the end of her junior year, Aileen realized that she would have to keep her eyes open, knock on doors, and ask a lot of questions. Through a high school business course, she signed up for three weeks of summer enrichment classes at a nearby college and lived in the dorms there. She felt shy and desperately homesick, but the experience gave her insight into what she wanted: a college where she could live at home and commute.

Some students find themselves showered with information about how to get to college. Many others, like Aileen, have to rely on their own courage and determination to obtain the facts they need. In this chapter, they tell their stories of how they did that, and give you their advice on what to try, to get the support you need.

It's hard to think concretely about going to college unless you get the chance to see one. Even if you *don't want* to go to college close to home, you can gather important information about what it's like, by taking a look at the campuses near where you live. It may only show you what you *don't* want in a college, but that's good to know, too.

For example, by trying out a summer session in the dorms after eleventh grade, Aileen found out that she preferred to take on the challenges of college work while living at home with her family.

>> I was too shy. I always kept on my own, and if you want to go away for college you have to be kind of outgoing. It really wasn't for me. Moving out, I'm not ready for that stuff right now. I just go to class, get out, come to work, go back to school if I have to at night, and that's it. I don't make it a social life, I just go to school. That's the only way I know I could make it. - AILEEN

Karen Powless, an Ojibwe-Cree Indian living in Stillwater, Oklahoma, worked for seventeen years after high school, and started a family. Then— almost on a fluke—she found herself on a college campus and got inspired to sign up for a class.

>> I graduated from high school and for many years I was a waitress. And then I was a firefighter with the Cheyenne Arapahoe fire suppression program, and they needed an EMT. I didn't have my driver's license, and at that time I was going across the border to Canada to visit my family, so I needed an ID. So I went to OSU Oklahoma City and took the placement test, just so I could have an ID. (It worked, I got across the border!) And I signed up for one class, Student Success Strategies, for students that have been out for a number of years.

The first three semesters, I just took one class. And I received A's, which was totally shocking to me. I always say I'm a late bloomer, but at least I'm blooming! - KAREN

Like many urban high schools, the one Niema Jordan attended did not have enough college counselors to help all students. So she set out to look for answers and determine which colleges would make a good match for her.

》 I didn't have a big sister or brother or even a cousin to go to and say, "What did you do in order to get in?" So I read other people's accounts in books. I looked at the admissions websites for the different colleges. Maybe you have an ideal college in mind—that's where some people start out. I know people who were like, "I want to go to an Ivy League." So they went online and researched all the requirements, and that's how they planned out their high school career. For me, it wasn't necessarily that I wanted to get into a certain school. I just wanted to get into college.

Things don't always fall in your lap, you know what I'm saying? Like, everybody's not searching you out. Everybody's not looking for you. You have to take the initiative. - NIEMA

Keep going back to the guidance office. If one person doesn't help you, ask another.

Aileen grew discouraged at the lack of encouragement from her high school guidance office. They didn't really know her, and they seemed to have already decided that she shouldn't go to college.

》 The middle of your senior year, you have to see your counselor to see where you're standing at, your academic standing. That's when she just told me what I was going to do. She said, "Oh, just go to like a trade school, just get a certificate, or go to a community college where you get all the basics." I said, "No, I don't want to do that, I want to go to college." She said, "No, you're not going to college, you can't apply." I'm like, "Why not?" She said, "They're just not going to accept you, you're not ranked in the top tenth of the high school." - AILEEN

But she recalls another counselor, who advised her when she first arrived at the school.

》 It was a different counselor, not the one that was assigned to me, but she was the only one there when my mother registered us. And she was like, "If you pass all your classes this year you'll be a senior next year." And she kept on telling me that. I'm like, "Okay, if I can do this, I'll be a senior" —so I did it. And that's what helped me. - AILEEN

Looking back, Aileen wishes that she had kept in touch with that counselor, who reached out to help her succeed. Many guidance offices have responsibility for so many students that they allow some to fall through the cracks. Going back again and again, and asking different people your questions about how to get to college, can help you find the one person who will connect with you.

Ask students who are already in college what you need to know.

You can find a lot of information just by talking to older students about the road to college. In her third year at Bowling Green State University, near the Ohio town where she grew up, Stephanie Serda started thinking about how to get her younger brother J.R. to apply there, too. A junior in high school, he was planning to follow in their father's footsteps as a construction worker.

>> His counselor told him that there wasn't a major for him in college if he wanted to go into construction. And this made me pretty upset. He's always had to work extra hard in school, and I think that's something that discouraged him from going to college. And it seemed to me the counselor was like, "Well, he's not college bound," you know. I was like, "J.R., I know for a fact they have construction management courses here, and it's not just one course you can take, it's a major!" He's like, "Really?" If I hadn't gone here, would my brother know that there is construction management? No. And it's a big difference for him, because it tells him that if he wants to go into construction he doesn't just have to go to trade school. He can go to university. When you earn a degree in something, you have the opportunity to get a higher position, whereas if you go to trade school, you might just be a laborer the whole time. – STEPHANIE

Karen Powless, the student from Oklahoma, only found out about financial aid possibilities by talking with other students, after she had already paid full price for the first few courses she took.

>> My parents had told me, "If you want to go to college, you're going to have to pay for it yourself." So I did not know about financial aid, I did not know about Pell Grants or loans or scholarships, and I did not know about different schools having different tuition rates. I was paying sky-high just for one class. Then I heard people say, "Oh, I got my financial aid check," and

I said, "What's that?" This is when I was still taking one class a semester, 'cause I was paying for it. They said, "You're not getting financial aid? Go sign up for it!" - KAREN

Now that she is a student leader on campus, Karen looks for every chance to tell prospective students about ways to help pay for college.

》 I have Pell Grant scholarships, and I just recently started taking loans. I was going to try to graduate debt-free, but if the student needs loans, go for it. Just don't get into the credit-card deal—there goes your credit, bad credit.

I really encourage people to try out for scholarships, even if it's an essay they ask for. A one- or two-page essay—I will do it any day! It's worth trying; that piece of paper is worth $1500! My advice: Save your essays on a disk, 'cause you can tweak them a little bit and re-use them, you know. - KAREN

Make a list of your interests, then connect them up to college.

Like Stephanie's brother J.R., you may have some interest that you could follow up by studying it in college. Niema, for example, thought about the things she most enjoyed doing, as she looked for colleges. It occurred to her that she might study for a career based on her love of writing.

》 My mom didn't sit me down and say, "Be a journalist!" It's just something that came to me—my passion is for writing, and I thought, "Okay, how do I write and get paid at the same time?" You always have to search things out and look for a connection and network. I didn't know about Northwestern University. I was looking for schools to apply to, and I could have very well only applied to schools that I had heard of before. I could have been like, "Well, all I know are University of California, so I'm staying here and going to a U.C." But I chose to ask other people, "Do you know anywhere that has a journalism program?" I went online: "journalism"—what comes up? - NIEMA

Once you get to college, Karen Powless found, your original interest might lead you into a completely different field. Karen started out by planning to train as an EMT or a paramedic, but later changed her mind. She received her two-year degree in crime victim survivors services, then she went on for a bachelors degree at the state university. She plans to go for the highest degree, a Ph.D., in her quest to help people with their troubles.

» My B.A. will be in sociology with a minor in women's studies. My masters, I want to do in social work, and my doctorate either in sociology or grief. I really would like to go into the study of grief, to have a hand in helping people put it in a perspective that's dealable for them. And with my degree, first of all, I want to go back to Canada, work with my people. – KAREN

You can also choose a college without knowing what you want to study there.

You don't need to have a career in mind in order to pick the right college or even the right courses. Niema talks about how to look around for a place where you can explore all the possibilities once you get there.

» So you don't know what you're looking for in a school? You always know *something*. You know that you can't stand to be cold, so don't choose a school on the East Coast and don't come to Chicago! You know that much already! If you like to draw, make sure they have art classes. You may love to dance, but if a school doesn't have a good dance program, is there a good dance company around that school you could join in your off time? Well then, that gives that school a bonus.

Look at what you're interested in—it doesn't always have to be the academics, because when you get to school, your life is not going to be centered around your books. If you don't know what you want to do with your life later, you know what you enjoy doing with your life now. Look at that, as far as how to choose colleges. – NIEMA

Keep your family in the loop.

If your family has no experience with college so far, they will need to learn about it right along with you. What you find out may differ from what they expect, so you will have some talking to do together.

Rosa Fernández arrived in New York City from the Dominican Republic as a teenager and attended a small public school for immigrant students. She and her classmates soon realized that the choices for college in America did not reflect the family and cultural traditions they were familiar with.

» There's a big difference that has to do with the American concept of "going away" to college. In the Dominican Republic, students live at home, they take classes maybe in a big city and they go back to their houses in the little towns where they live. It's nothing like living away from home. At my school I knew many students whose parents were saying, "No, you're not going anywhere else, you're staying in the city," so they weren't able to pick and choose what they wanted. – ROSA

Rosa worked hard and rose to the top of her high school class, and by senior year she was applying to a number of selective private colleges, almost none of them close to home.

» It's important to know early on what you want, so you can start talking to your parents and getting the information, taking the right academic steps to go on. Once you know the difference between certain kinds of colleges, you start to sensitize your parents to what the choices are, and what is out there. You start being able to say, "Okay, what do I need to do to be able to go to that college?" – ROSA

Aileen Rosario's parents also spoke no English, and they knew very little about the path to college. Aileen's high school did not make the effort to inform them, so she had to find ways to share what she was learning.

» The process would have been easier for me if the school had reached out to my parents, or somebody in my house. Give them tools that are useful, like how to go visit a college, find the majors you're interested in, fill out the application itself, find a recommendation. Getting my parents really interested in helping me go to college was hard because nobody knew about college. They all had kids to take care of, and everybody was in their own little world. – AILEEN

As they worked to find out everything they needed to know, Aileen and Rosa both faced real obstacles. They put a lot of effort into getting ready and finding the path to college that would work for them. Part of their success was simply keeping their family members informed and aware of their desires. In the next chapter, students will tell about how they made a network of people who cared about their futures, and who helped them on the way to college.

4

Support Networks

How friends, parents, teachers, and others can help

*E*ver since he was a young boy, Eric Polk had his head in a book. Even his friends who hung out on the streets of East Nashville told him that he would go to college one day, without a doubt. When they went off to party, they called his mother to make sure Eric went home instead of getting in trouble.

Those friendships were just some of the relationships that supported Eric's progress at home, at school, and after school. His great-aunt Rachel talked him through an emotional breakdown in his tenth-grade year. His English teacher, Miss Quick, took his questions and his academic ambitions seriously. And at his internship with a community nonprofit organization, his two supervisors became like father and brother to him, coaching him into a leadership role out in the world.

Now that Eric has actually made it to Wake Forest University, he often thinks of how each of these people helped him to get there—by believing in him, encouraging him, and holding out opportunities for him to expand his horizons. They connected him into a network that keeps on supporting him through his hard times and celebrating his successes.

>> I am below the poverty level and I'm gonna need help! Across all lines, you never know who can help you—and later on in life, they can still help. If you shut out people, you're going to be by yourself, and you don't want to be by yourself. Network, learn, connect, and talk to people. Tap into some of those resources, because they are resources! Then the better off you'll be. You can't go through high school staying to yourself—colleges these days are looking for well-rounded people, so get out of the shell, put yourself out there. - ERIC

Your world, too, may already contain many people who can help you along the road to college. Finding and reaching out to them may be the most important thing you can do during your high school years.

Even if your parents didn't go to college, your family has experience and knowledge that can help you up the ladder.

Eric suffered from depression in ninth and tenth grades. He felt like an outsider at the large high school where he was a newcomer. When he lost hope and faith that he would ever find friends and success, close family members came to his support.

>> My great-aunt called me and said, "I'm really worried about you. As much as I want to tell you to do this, do that, and believe in this, believe in that, I'm going to try to tell you to believe in yourself, and do things that you feel like are important for you to do. So what's the best thing for Eric to do?" I was like, "To leave?" She's like, "Okay, now! How are you going to leave?" I was like, "I'm going to go to college." And she's like, "Well, how are you going to go to college?" "I guess by getting good grades." "But *how* are you going to get good grades?" "By working for them!" "Oh! So if you work for it and you get good grades and you do what you're supposed to be doing, and graduate, that's your ticket to get out of there!" I just started laughing. Because she basically broke it down, "Well, how are you going to do that?" Everything started to change from that moment on. I was going to be me. – ERIC

Hazel Janssen went through a hard time, too, after she dropped out of high school. She struggled to keep her balance in the adult world. It was her mother who helped Hazel get back on track without going back to the big school she hated. Her mom discovered a special "opportunity high school" in Denver, which offered both high school and college courses.

>> For a while I was living with my boyfriend, who my parents did not approve of, and money was very tight. I wasn't working at the time, and I wasn't going to school, so I had very little contact with my parents at that point. And then I decided, "I have to stop this, because I can't just live here forever, not work and not go to school and not ever talk to my family again, that's ridiculous." So I went and I talked to my family and we discussed me moving back in with them, and my mom said, "Well, you can stay here rent free, but you have to go to school."

> My mom would constantly bombard me with little tidbits of informa-tion, like, "You know, Hazel, high school dropouts make 30 percent less than those who have graduated, and when you have a college degree, you can make twice as much as someone who just graduated from high school!" She would try and remind me that if I wanted my future to be semi-okay and not just spend the rest of my life working in a Burger King or an ice cream store, then I'd have to pursue higher learning. It's impor-tant to know that if you drop out of high school, you can still get a diploma and you can still go to college. It's not the end. – HAZEL

Niema's mother never went to college; instead, at seventeen she put aside her scholarship to Spelman College to care for her newborn daugh-ter. Perhaps because of that, Niema always heard her mother's drumbeat: Work hard, stay organized, and you will go to college when your time comes. "It wasn't an option not to," says Niema, even though her family lived near the bottom of the economic ladder. Her mother's determination helped her stay focused and keep her dream in sight.

Jackie didn't really start planning seriously for college until after she graduated. Her father, who had always wanted to do something better with his life, kept pressing her to talk to the admissions counselor at the nearby university. His encouragement got her there.

》 I'm like, "A university?" I tried to get him to let me go to the community college first, and he's like, "No, I know you can do it." I decided, well, I might as well try this. So I went and talked to a really good college coun-selor at Colorado University in Denver, and he helped me get the Governor's Opportunity Scholarship. It's a four-year full ride to help the Hispanic/Latino people who are getting in for the first time. That was a great thing they have. I was really thrilled. – JACKIE

Teachers and coaches are a great link to college—their job is to help you succeed.

When she entered high school, Niema got another important boost, in a leadership class taught by a young African-American man. He had grown up in Oakland, too, and gone on to the University of California. He did not let up for a second with his message: Take responsibility for your own success.

》 This is something he instilled in us: A lot of people want power in their lives, and control over things, and money, and success, and they go about this by different routes. But you have to think about what actually gives you power.

We had to know all the UC's in the University of California system and at least nine California State universities. And we had to be able to name three private colleges and at least two other community colleges in our area. He said, "You can't possibly go somewhere you don't know exists." When you don't realize there's something better out there for you, or you feel that the something better is just too good for you, nothing is going to change. People don't know that they have the power to change their situation. If they've seen someone else do it before, that's how they know it's possible.

So you're presented with a path. One, you have to figure out how to empower the people who are on the same level as you. And two, you have to figure out a way to make the people who have more power than you *care* what's going on with your life. – NIEMA

If you think of the adults at your school as people with interests of their own, it makes it easier to connect with them. Your conversations with teachers before or after class give them a sense of who you are as an individual. You can build strong, long-lasting friendships with them, and when it comes time to apply to college, they will be ready with advice and recommendations.

》 Get to know your teachers; I really believe they are there to help you. Especially with what they're getting paid—they're there because they want to be, trust me! Once you get that, you pretty much feel respect. Teachers are people too; they have lives outside of school, and they will surprise you. – ERIC

From their own personal college experiences, and from helping many other students get there, teachers are a storehouse of insights and information that can help you. Don't be shy to ask.

» They've dealt with students coming in before you who have maybe had struggles similar to yours, who are off in college now. They can connect you with those students, or tell you what they've observed. – NIEMA

Stephen, a football player in high school, found that his coaches also gave him important practical and emotional support.

» Coaches definitely helped out a lot. You could talk to them as people; they worked with you; they knew about your family; you could call them on the phone. In my small town, the coaches would give you a ride home if you needed it.

My power lifting coach was actually also my algebra teacher, so he always pushed me to do good: "Make sure you get your homework in, make sure you do all these great things." He expected a lot of his students, but nothing that couldn't be accomplished. He would get up in your face if he had to: "Dammit son, I'm not asking you to nail Jello to a tree!" He would tell you how it is. But when you went home at night you'd know he loved you and wanted the best for you. – STEPHEN

Find places outside school where you can gain experience and work alongside adults.

Aileen Rosario was lost in the crowd at a high school where her guidance counselor didn't see her potential. She needed help and she found it. She took a business class that got her an internship at a community organization, and she made friends with the three women who supervised her. Aileen came to regard these mentors as "my three mothers."

» I started working here around the end of September my senior year. I really trusted my employer, Anna. When I was telling her what was going on in school, the first question she asked me was, "What college are you applying to?" That's when I really started to think about college, because here, they were not happy to think that I was not going to college. They really pushed me, like, "You're going to college, apply to colleges!" They all gave me different ideas of what I could do, and they asked me what was the one thing that I wanted to do. I said I wanted to be a lawyer. They said,

"You could do it, you just have to go to school for it!" That's when I started thinking about the options I had, and I started researching college.

My three mothers at work helped me with the whole applications process. I consider them my parents in a way, 'cause I can't go to my actual parents and talk about it. When I have a problem and I come to them, they understand me, and they help me fix it. – AILEEN

In eleventh grade, Eric Polk got involved with Community Impact, a nonprofit organization that trains young people to be leaders in their neighborhoods. That experience gave Eric skills and self-confidence, but also it helped him think very differently about life after high school.

》 It was life-changing work. I gained so much knowledge. I'm a high school student, I'm seventeen years old, and I'm writing grants! I can honestly sit here and say that I helped to raise over $380 million, in government money, to help employ young people in the East Nashville community.

The staff at Community Impact was so small, you pretty much knew everybody, and everybody knew you. It wasn't like "I'm the adult and you're the young person"—if I had something to say, it was taken as if the executive director was saying it himself. It's like, "If we don't have young people on our staff, that contradicts everything we stand for." I have a voice, and people take it seriously. So I started saying everything exactly how I felt, and it felt pretty darn good!

One day I walked into the office and my boss John had this really serious expression on his face. And he looked at me, he's like, "Have you ever thought about going to Wake Forest University?" I was like, "Are you serious? Do you know where I'm graduating from? I don't think that's possible!" Because I felt like I was not prepared to go. The quality of the education at my high school is just not there.

So John sat down and he talked to me. He was like, "I want you to think about it, go and research Wake Forest, and see if that would be a place you would be interested in." So the program director from Community Impact brought me here for a campus visit to check it out, and I liked what I saw. John was like, "Okay, now. If we could just turn the key and open the door, would you go through it?"

I was like, "It sounds like it's going to be really hard." But I looked at these two men who had pushed me so much to do all the things I've done, sitting there saying, "We know this is a good fit for you." When you're presented with that type of confidence, it's hard to say no. I said, "I think I can do it." He was like, "That's all I need to know." – ERIC

A summer program is a great way to test out the college experience.

Rosa Fernández took part in an Upward Bound program on a college campus near her home in the Bronx, New York the summer after her junior year. She took high school courses that she needed in order to graduate, and lived in campus dorms for the whole summer. In New Jersey, Aileen applied for a similar opportunity at a local college, but she wanted one that let her come home and spend time with family and friends on the weekends. These programs come in all types, and many have full scholarships for low-income or minority students.

» It was free, and I decided to go just to see the experience. We stayed on campus for three weeks, but we came home Thursdays and went back on Sunday evenings. We took college classes in critical thinking, public speaking, English, and math. If you passed the class, you would get college credit, but if you didn't, you just went there. They gave us two or three hours tutoring, so we could do all our homework, and we went to events. It was a good experience. – AILEEN

In Texas, Stephen Torres spent an intensive week on campus, exploring his interests and making new connections.

» After my tenth-grade year, I went to a summer program at the University of Texas called Minority Introduction to Engineering. I came to campus and stayed in a dorm for a week, I worked with engineering students to do some cool things. I was like, "Wow, this is what computer programming is like, this is what graphic design is like—this is what you can be when you grow up!" We went and visited different businesses around the Austin area. It was really cool, and I loved it. I remember being very empowered at the time. "Yeah, Stephen, that's great, you're interested in engineering, but you also write really well, you can also lead a discussion really well," people began realizing that in me. When I came here two years later there were students that still remembered me. - STEPHEN

Now that he is a student leader at the university, Stephen has helped pass that favor along. With others at a student organization, he launched a program in which Latino high school students with many different interests come to campus to discuss cultural identity and leadership.

If your high school counselors aren't encouraging you, visit your local community college or community center and talk with the counselors there.

Most community colleges are eager to talk with potential students and help them figure out a course of study that matches their interests. So if your high school guidance office does not seem to take you seriously, or just can't find the time to help you, try making an appointment directly with a college admissions or counseling office. Niema, who comes from a state with a large community college system, has seen that work for friends who had a low grade-point average.

》 A lot of community colleges have feeder programs into the state colleges and universities. You can basically chart out with them whatever classes you need to be taking right now, in order to get accepted into the four-year college. - NIEMA

Community centers also have counselors who are there to talk to youth. You can meet a mentor anywhere, Aileen says, not just at a place where you work or go to school.

》 It's good to have somebody that you know you could go to, no matter what, with any type of question. Just somebody you trust that you could talk to. There are some places, like community centers, that have a lot of mentors. Or maybe your friend has a mother that goes to college, and she won't mind if you ask a question. Or a family friend that's been to college and knows a couple of things. - AILEEN

Students who are the first in their family to go to college need a lot of support, because they are pioneers exploring a new environment and new experiences. No one can do it alone, so don't hesitate to reach out and ask others for what you need.

The next chapter focuses on some of the stereotypes that can prevent people from having access to college. In it, students describe ways that you can make sure your high school, your teachers, and your counselors work to support you, rather than hold you back.

5

Stand Up for Your Education

How to defy stereotypes and low expectations

Stephanie Serda's family did not interfere with her plans to go to college, but they didn't expect it, either. Now that she is at a state university in Ohio, she worries about whether her two younger brothers will be prepared to follow in her footsteps. Because her brothers started out on the non-college track, she thinks, they may not have the chance to take challenging courses that will get them ready for college.

» I really want to see them come to college and it's hard for me to not pres-sure them. I know my parents don't pressure them at all, because they didn't pressure me. So I encouraged them and pushed them a little. I was telling them, "Come on, guys, just study harder, 'cause if you do good in those classes, they'll put you back up into regular or college prep classes.
— STEPHANIE

Stephanie is right to worry. If you want to go to college, right from the start you have to raise your voice, ask for what you need, and keep your eyes open about what classes and opportunities your high school offers you. Somebody may have stuck a "non-college" label on you because of your previous grades, or because of stereotypes about your background, your skin color, or your interests.

You do not have to accept those negative labels. On the contrary, many colleges will value the fact that you have the courage and strength to go after your goals without the resources that many students take for granted. If you make good choices and stand up for yourself, you can go after the preparation you need. In this chapter, students share their stories of how they fought for their education—and they give you ideas of how to do so yourself.

Even if your class or your school is not "college prep," you can stand out by focusing on college.

Eric Polk went to a very low-performing high school in Nashville, Tennessee, where sometimes it seemed as if nobody cared about college at all. Many teachers did not have enough training in their fields, and classroom behavior often went completely out of control. However, Eric felt that his classmates and teachers were actually just as smart as anyone else. To him, they just seemed discouraged, as if they were brought down by the low expectations that the rest of society had for them.

》 It took a while to recognize that I didn't have to be that way. The way I was brought up, I was like, "I'm not going to ruin myself to that, I refuse to lower myself to that." So I will be a geek, I will be a nerd, but I will not be a thug, I'm not going to be a drug dealer, I'm not going to be any of that! You can basically call me whatever name you want to. And it took me actually coming out and saying that. It was like, "I just choose not to. Now what? You don't like me? I don't care if you like me or not! I'm still going to be here, I'm still breathing, I'm still alive."

Kids were playing around in a lot of classes, throwing paper balls and whatnot, and the teacher's just standing there. I was like, "If I'm sitting here and I got my book open, you're a teacher, you can talk to me, I don't care what they do. Put them out if you have to; if you're going to teach, I'm here. I'm taking notes, I'm reading, I've done my homework, I'll pay attention." I was like, "I'm not going to focus on what other people think of me. I won't be defined by what they want me to be. I define myself." - ERIC

Since the classroom environment made it hard to focus, Eric began to seek out extra help from teachers after class.

》 I would go and clarify things: "I didn't understand what you meant by blah blah blah." Or say, "I'm sorry you couldn't finish your lesson today, is there anything from this lesson that I need to know about, that's going to be on the test?" - ERIC

Eric did not start off with many advantages, but he had a sense of his own worth. He made the best of what he had, pushed to find out what he needed to know, and stood up for himself and his education.

If a teacher seems to have low expectations of you, tell them you deserve more.

Stephen Torres played a lot of sports in high school. He was placed in the typical college-prep courses, but he noticed that other athletes often didn't get the same encouragement.

>> I hated reading—it was boring, as opposed to going out with friends. One of the jokes for me and some of my friends in high school, was like, "Man, if I only opened a book I could be so smart!" Some of my friends had the opportunity to move on to college, but the vast majority didn't. - STEPHEN

Stereotypes about students often show up in what teachers expect from them in their class work, Stephen noticed. Confronting that bias takes courage, but you may not be the only one who benefits when you stand up for yourself. Students who come after you will have a better chance, once teachers realize the wrong that prejudice can do them.

>> The first paper that I wrote for my English teacher, she actually gave it back to me and said, "These are good ideas, but I don't think you wrote it." I'm like, "What are you talking about, what's your problem?" and she's like, "I know about you; yes, you're a smart kid but you didn't write this paper." She would often say things like that I was the loudest kid in the entire hall-way, that you could always hear my voice over everyone else's. So with me being an athlete, me being loud and obnoxious at times, it was, "No, you can't write well."

I was pretty pissed off about the whole thing, and my mom was extremely upset and came and talked to her. With the next two papers I had written, the teacher ended up realizing that okay, you don't have to be a complete dumb-ass to be an athlete. She gave me a lot of respect after that moment. I love her, I still go back and see her now. But I remember we got off on that shaky foot, and she didn't know much about me. - STEPHEN

If you are still learning English, don't let anyone block your path to college.

As an immigrant student at a San Francisco high school, Naixing Lei had an enormous challenge in just learning English. Even though he had taken difficult courses in his Chinese high school, in America he found himself in low-level classes, along with other students new to the language. None of his teachers encouraged him to prepare for college, Naixing says.

>> At the beginning I did very poorly in all my classes, especially in English class. I couldn't advance from that class. The only class that gave me satisfaction was math, because when I was in China the math levels were pretty advanced, compared to here in the United States. In middle school, they already teach advanced level math. – NAIXING

The fact that you are learning English now should not stop your college plans. Rosa Fernández started ninth grade in New York City with no English, and for the first two years she pushed hard to immerse herself academically in her new language. Even though she felt discouraged at times, she says it is worth the effort to take the hardest courses you can manage.

>> You need to expose yourself to the language even if you're afraid of it and you don't know it. Just go out there and take courses, ask questions, listen to people around you talking. I recommend taking all courses in English if you have a good background in your own language and you are willing to work hard. I'm not saying you should not appreciate your language, but courses like history and English—even if you have low English skills—allow you to read in the language and build vocabulary and listen to teachers give lectures. It just takes time and a good dictionary. – ROSA

Each student learns differently, and if adults don't trust that you can do well, you still deserve the chance to try. Like Rosa, you can defend your right to take difficult courses.

>> I wanted to get into a history course that I could not get into because I was a first-year student. I spoke to the teacher and counselor and explained, "Well, I may not have been here for a year, and I may not be able to understand everything in the course. But I think that by taking this risk I will

learn a lot more, because I will be listening and writing and reading in English for a longer time." They believed in the principle that students should be taking both Spanish courses and English—kind of a transition time. I think that educators should be aware that this doesn't work for every student. – ROSA

Rosa's school performance did get better over time, as her English improved. When she applied to a number of selective colleges during her senior year, she used several strategies to show them that she could do well there.

» If you're applying to college and they see that since ninth grade your grades have been improving, it's a sign that you're learning the language, you're assimilating, and that takes time. It's not going to count against you. I also took the TOEFL* and the SAT Subject Test* in Spanish, so they can see I can dominate in my own language. You need to tell college admissions, some way, that you can do the work in English but you didn't do very well on the SATs for x or y reasons.

At the beginning I got the lowest score in the whole SAT program, but over time, after a year, I got higher and higher. I was taking a preparation course, but also spending time understanding English in my regular courses. I improved 300 points—that was really an accomplishment. I cried that day. – ROSA

Students of color, or those without economic privilege, often have to push back against low expectations.

Now that he is a student at the University of Texas, Stephen still stops by his father's little corner barbershop in Austin every couple of weeks. He feels pride when he sees his father's dealings with clients who come from very different backgrounds.

» The people who walk in there can be from all walks of life, and he can communicate wonderfully with them, whether they're recent immigrants or hard-working construction workers or university professors. It's a pretty integrated Mexican-white community. He has some understanding but not the education, but he can talk to pretty much anyone. And I think that that

---

* Test of English as a Foreign Language.
* A subject-area standardized test given by the College Board organization.

is something I try to bring to the college campus. You can be active in the black community and the Mexican community and advocate for social change in a number of different communities. - STEPHEN

Ever since he was in high school, Stephen has seen the ways that black and Latino students do not get the encouragement and advantages that their white classmates experience on the way to college. He noticed it most on the playing fields, he says.

» We played together, we ate together, we had grown up our entire lives together. But we knew that wasn't the power that was going to play out on the football field. Even though the black running back would get all the way down to the goal line, a lot of times the ball would be passed to a white receiver or to a white running back for the touchdown. My junior year we made it really deep into the playoffs, and it was odd—the understanding amongst the team about who was going to be given time for interviews whenever the news crews came around. The people that the coaches think are more likely to go to college—that are more likely to be presentable, if you want to say that, on TV—they were always white students. And as football players we understood that, white students included. The same way, there was still the reality that there was not going to be a black homecoming queen. - STEPHEN

Stephen noticed that the bias came out in different ways at school— sometimes social and sometimes academic. Like his father, he maintained good relationships across different groups. This helped him learn about the issues he wanted to study in college, and made him determined to work for social change.

» Luckily for me, I was able to play both roles. I could hang out with the athletes and the more black and brown students, but also have a certain amount of trust and have intellectual conversations with the white students in the class-room. The intellectual conversations I had with black and brown students did focus on the inequality of the school system, on "Why is it this way?" I think those conversations, more than anything, played a large role in my path here in college. I was offered an opportunity. I'm representing so many others who could easily be in this position, but for a lot of reasons aren't. - STEPHEN

Students who are the first in their family to strive for higher education are pushing back against enormous social forces. They will likely encounter situations that offer them wonderful support, and also situations that are challenging and discouraging. Part of your job is to keep your balance as you seek your own path, and maintain a strong sense of self-worth. In the next chapter, students explain how they found support and did just that.

Stay True to You

How to keep your social and emotional balance

By the time Joshua Cryer turned eighteen, he says, "I knew what was right and wrong and what I wanted to do with my life." His single mother, who worked as a hotel housekeeper, brought him up to rely on common sense.

When he was younger, the family did "a lot of moving and bustling around from house to house," Joshua says. In his fifth-grade year, they moved into low-income apartments in a mostly white school district, and he had to make all new friends at his new middle school. He started playing sports; by high school, he was a star athlete in football, track, swimming, wrestling, and pole vaulting, and he had joined a number of clubs. Everyone knew him, and he felt their support.

But as an African-American from a family without much money, Joshua felt two ways about his upper-middle-class, largely white environment. He began dating a white girl from a college-educated family, soaking up the inside knowledge his girlfriend had about how to succeed in life. "She had that exposure to professionalism: 'Here's success, this is how you do it, this is what happens,'—things that I didn't have. Being with her, I was exposed to those type of things, which in turn helped me to get where I am now, I'm positive."

At the same time, he couldn't help noticing that his girlfriend's relatives did not believe that Joshua would have a successful future like their own.

>> When we were face to face, they were always positive. But I could hear them in the other room, or maybe they didn't know I was standing there. Some of the negative things that they were saying just gave me more motivation to continue in the path that I was going on, so that I could set a better example for students that would come behind me, so that people would look at those students and treat them as equals. We're people, and that's it. - JOSHUA

STAY TRUE TO YOU **41**

Joshua's story illustrates the complicated feelings that come up for students who are the first in their family to go for a college education. Of course, you need all the support you can get from your friends, family, and your community. On the other hand, you may have the sense that people are looking at you as a "special case"—or that you have to try even harder than most people just to gain admission into a group that may not completely want to include you. Finally, when your time comes to go off to college, you may have mixed feelings about leaving behind the friends and familiar supports of home.

In the stories that follow, students talk about how they dealt with those difficult feelings.

Starting in ninth grade, Eric Polk did so well in high school that he felt as though other students did not want him as a friend.

>> Freshman year was so hard, I hated it. I was wanting to be like everyone else, but at the same time I didn't. That made me so weird. I would get in the chemistry or bio class and ace everything, and like: "Eric, would you please explain to your peers why this is such and such?" "Okay, well this is the DNA molecule . . ." And people would just look like, "Teacher's pet. Nerd. Why do you know this stuff?" I hated myself. I would criticize myself because they criticized me. - ERIC

To relieve his stress and sadness, Eric turned to music, and joined the marching band. After years of playing his trombone with that group, he was amazed to find his social situation improving dramatically—without his having to give up his academic goals.

>> At the end of sophomore year, I tried out for head drum major, and I made it! And instantly, just like that, everybody at school was like, "You're so cool, you do pretty good, could you help me with my homework?" All of a sudden, I'm popular, and not understanding why. I still don't get it! But that didn't change what my mentality was and what I was trying to do. - ERIC

Naixing Lei, too, had trouble fitting in as a newcomer to his San Francisco high school. For one thing, his limited English made it hard for him to join classmates in tasks that required discussion.

>> Sometimes when the teachers arrange the group discussions, it is inevitable that the English speakers will feel like, "Don't be in our group," and they will see you as trouble. I didn't feel angry, because that is natural. It's natural. The only thing that I would tell myself is to work harder and be able to speak like they do one day. - NAIXING

To help himself feel less discouraged, Naixing called on the traditional beliefs of his family's Chinese culture.

>> Remember the old Buddhist saying: "The best way to predict the future is to create it." I learn a lot from the old sayings, because although it's kind of short, it contains a lot of meanings and knowledge, and teaches you how to behave, how to think. I really apply them to my life. - NAIXING

It helps to find friends who want to go to college, too.

In fact, step by step, Naixing did create his own future. Once he gathered enough courage to speak to his high school classmates, he made new friends who gave him important support in his journey toward college.

>> We like to play tennis, and read comic books in Chinese. Some of the students speak Chinese too, they came here when they were eight or nine. Most of them go to college now, and some of them were able to get into a four-year university. They are friendly, they have good habits—don't go to school late, and respect the teachers, and do the homework, be good students. There's a Chinese proverb, "You know from his friends what kind of person someone is." So, for instance, if that person hangs out with bad guys, you will immediately know that person is not a good person. But in contrast, if that person is hanging out with people who get all A's, and are hardworking, good students, you know he is good. - NAIXING

Although Aileen has a shy nature, she too found high school friends who shared her hopes to attend college. Watching them turn a dream into reality helped her believe that she could do it, too.

>> There was one junior already talking about college, and a couple of girls I always talked to, both seniors like me. They were thinking about college but they were not sure what they wanted to do with their lives. One of

them applied to a trade school, and another one really wanted to go to college to be a doctor. I only had gym with her, but we became really close friends, and after school, we talked on the phone. We still hang out sometimes. She got accepted to Rutgers University. She started a semester late, because she did get pregnant her senior year in high school. But that didn't stop her, she still went to school with the baby and everything. So that was really like, "Wow, if she could do it, I could do it, 'cause I don't have kids!" - AILEEN

Later, Aileen's own success in college inspired her closest sister to try for the same thing. After the birth of her baby, she decided to go back to school, and now she expects to receive an associates degree herself.

Eric found a new close friend when he took up marching band. Knowing someone else who cared about doing well academically made him feel less alone as he worked toward a future at college. "My friend Earl was a striver," he says. "So it was just kind of finding my place."

Your success matters even to others who are not going to college.

As the sixth of seven children, Aileen could always tell how much it mattered to her parents and older sisters that she make it to a new level of opportunity.

» My parents really didn't bother with my brothers and sisters, 'cause they all had dropped out of high school. But they saw that I was headed the right way—like I hadn't gotten left back in school, and I was doing real good— and they persuaded me. By telling me, "Oh, you have to go to college," they felt that was going to keep me in the right direction. They're happy that I'm in college. My older sisters are happy about it, too. Every time I talk to them, they tell me, "Oh, please, don't get pregnant, please, please, don't end up like me!" - AILEEN

Stephen Torres held his church community in the back of his mind, hoping to make its members proud of his accomplishment.

» I worked for my church in high school, I was active in the church community and the youth group and things like that. So all the little old ladies and the old people that grew up in East Austin and have been there for quite some time, they looked to me as someone young but someone who was respectable.

I, of course, looked up to them, for their wisdom and things they could offer. I think that was the place I could give back and know that whatever I was doing was for something positive, for a solid community-type feeling. – STEPHEN

Sometimes you'll need to walk away from people and situations that can keep you from your college goals.

Aileen remembers the point when she decided to break up with her high school boyfriend because she found his attitude about college too discouraging. It was not the first time she had realized that the people she hung out with could have an impact on her long-term goals.

》 He had his mind set already, "I'm not college material, I don't want to go to college." I don't want to be with somebody that doesn't want to do something with his life, you know, so I just got away from him. You have to be careful who you talk to. They discourage you, some people. Even though they say they're your friend, they might be jealous of you. They're like, "Oh, college is not for you, you got to have a job and get paid so good," you know.

You really have to think about who you're going to be friends with, how they're going to impact your life. I thought about everything, like "I'll talk to her, because she's more my type, she's more quiet, she's more into school." Some friends could be good or they could be a negative part of your life. Let's say you're not into smoking or something—if your friends smoke, you think it's cool, so you're going to do it too. What type of friends do you want to be seen with? – AILEEN

A cousin, four years older, had always been like a big sister to Stephanie, and up to a certain point Stephanie wanted to do everything just like her.

》 I've looked up to her my whole life. My grandmother babysat us before and after school growing up, so we were together all the time. She went to the same high school—she played soccer, I played basketball. And when I was in high school she had just graduated a little bit before, and she would hang out with the girls from the neighborhood, and it was a really fast life. I would hang out with her and have fun, going different places or whatever.

She didn't go to college. I'm not saying I don't look up to her anymore, 'cause I still do, but we just have gone totally different paths. Right now she has two kids, two different fathers, and she's married to the second. It's not that

I look down on it, but it's not where I want to be in four years, at all. It's crazy to think that up until that point I followed in her footsteps, and now—she looks up to me, because she knows she could have gone to college. - STEPHANIE

College brings you into a new social community, so look for one where you feel supported and valued.

Very few students at Niema's Oakland high school even considered leaving California for college. So when she applied to Northwestern University, near Chicago, she raised a few eyebrows. Was she putting old friendships behind her? Had she stopped caring about her family?

» Wanting to be around your friends can't be a reason to keep you from going to college, and it can't be the reason you go to college. If you're true friends, you'll be friends regardless. So if your best friend's the only reason you have to go to UCLA, you'll hate UCLA, because you don't spend every waking moment with your best friend. If your only reason for not going to college is because your best friend doesn't plan on going, then you're going to hate being stuck at home. - NIEMA

You will have many ways of keeping in touch with friends over a distance—phone calls, email, letters, photos, and visits can keep old friendships strong while you build new ones. Moving away might even give you a chance to see your friends on exciting new territory. Mike Morris, who played football in the state championships for his Mississippi high school, watched most of his friends be heavily recruited by their state university, which has a famous football team. For him, making a different choice was a matter of establishing his separate identity.

» Everyone went to Ole Miss, that was where you were expected to go. The coaches probably thought that was the best decision out of high school. I had an opportunity to go there, and I didn't feel that I should, because everyone wanted me to. I've always wanted to do the opposite thing the other person did. I like to be different. To me, it's being yourself, it's an identity. - MIKE

Though he moved many miles away, Mike did not forget his old friends and teammates. Later, when he played football for Brigham Young University in Utah, he imagined the pleasure of encountering them on the playing field.

>> One friend right now that's at Ole Miss is probably going to be a big star. He's a corner, he's very good. That's one reason I didn't want to go there, 'cause I've always wanted to play against him. That would be a dream. – MIKE

Karen Powless had already married and borne children when she decided to go to college, so she had a different problem when it came to leaving behind those she loved. In the tradition of Indian mothering, she took her five-year-old son with her, to the Oklahoma State University a half hour from her home.

>> I don't really feel the difficulties, because as a Native lady, we just take our children right along, and it's no big deal! When I have Native American Student Association meetings, normally I will try to get a sitter, but if I can't find it, I take him along. My son is like a shadow to me here on campus, everybody knows him. – KAREN

Because Karen does not drive a car, she and her child stay during the week in a rented place near campus, getting together with her husband on weekends. The family has adapted, she says.

>> My family made a decision that mom was going to seek a higher education, and there are some sacrifices that we do make. But we are both very independent people, and I think that really benefits us. He can cook, and he doesn't need to be by my side every day. – KAREN

While many students find it exciting to move to a new city, Aileen Rosario knew that she would miss the support of her family too much to consider going away to school.

>> I couldn't deal with the fact of being away from home, 'cause I never slept out of my house, away from my parents. So for me it didn't work, and I never thought about it again. It was like, "No, I'm not going away, I'm staying home." – AILEEN

Two years later, Aileen plans to continue commuting from home until she graduates from Montclair State University with her bachelors degree. Living with her family, she is keeping up her good grades and saving the earnings from her part-time job. By the time she applies to law school, she says, she will be ready to live on her own.

Enjoy where you are now—have fun, and take it one step at a time.

Between her schoolwork and her responsibilities as a student leader, Niema could have filled up every minute of high school with activities aimed at getting her into college. But she didn't like that idea.

>> You don't want to miss high school for the sake of getting into college. If you're spending your junior and senior year cooped up, bottled up, because you're so focused on getting into college, you're going to get into college and say, "What did I do with my life in high school?" You don't want to regret anything.

It's a really hard thing for some people to grasp, but you have to live at every moment. As long as you're not putting yourself in danger, go out and enjoy yourself. You do need to have priorities; you can't expect to be able to go to every single party that occurs and still hold your grades up. It comes with being able to balance, because living your life to the fullest means that you don't neglect any part of your life, you know? You can't lose yourself. You absorb everything and take in what you can, and you create the balance that makes your life most enjoyable. – NIEMA

Until he found music and the marching band, Eric felt isolated and unhappy as a high-achieving student in a low-achieving school. Life began to get better when he started to play music, dance, and open himself up to the pleasures of performing.

>> Find something that you like to do, and just strive to do that. You can build friendships in pretty much anything that you do. If you're in something that you really love to do, it fulfills something in your soul, it makes you smile, it relieves stress.

For me that was music, marching band. That changed around a lot of things. To see me—one of the people they would never expect to be a drum major—and find out, "This dude can dance, I didn't even know he had that side to him"—it was great!

That didn't change who I really was. And of course, some idiotic people were still picking on me, like, "You still reading all those things you used to read?" Mm-hmm! I still did my homework, I still studied, I still talked to the teachers, I still wrote poetry. But all of a sudden I had a balance—being popular and fitting in with the "in crowd," but also being able to maintain good grades in school. - ERIC

To deal with the stress of preparing for college in his new country, Naixing focuses on the simple act of breathing deeply.

》 To take a breath is important for a person, because if you get too stressful, it's not good for your physical health as well as your mental health. So always have time to study and time to relax. While you study, you have to focus on your studying. While you relax, just enjoy the time to relax. One thing at a time. - NAIXING

Niema found that taking time for her family was important in her senior year. As she juggled deadlines and home responsibilities, sometimes she felt that she could not wait to leave the nest and set out for an independent life as a college student. But now that she is at college, she looks back on that time with understanding and appreciation.

》 When I was applying to college, making sure my resumé was in order, studying for tests and writing papers and college applications, and I still had to wash dishes and take out the garbage—I was frustrated, like, "I don't want to take out the garbage!" And senior year there's this tension: "I have to hurry and get into college and, oh my grace, my mom's getting on my nerves, I don't want to deal with this"—and then Mom going, "My baby, where is she going? I need her!" So there's this pulling: You want to grow up, they want you to stay a kid.

And at times your parents tell you, "I don't care what you're doing, come sit down and talk to us." And you're like, "Oh no, I don't think you understand. You didn't go to college, you don't know the stress I'm under right now!" And they tell you, "I don't care if you're applying to go to an Ivy League, I don't care what you're doing. You come here and you sit down and you talk to us, or you eat with us." My mom doesn't care about the competition. She cares about keeping her family together. And the things that she was instilling in me, they help me now that I'm here. - NIEMA

The next chapter looks at how to stay organized and take care of all the details of your journey to college, so that you can enjoy your time in high school.

Taking Care of Business

How to keep it all organized and on time

*N*iema made her way through high school with college always on her to-do list.

>> It starts in ninth grade, when you're trying to get whatever classes are required. And then by tenth grade or junior year you start building up your resumé, and you're like rushing to join activities, because, "Oh, senior year they're going to look at this, what do colleges want?" So it's always been in my mind. I was doing everything I could get my hands on, I was overactive. Part of it was just me being an outgoing person, and another part of it was me going, "Oh my grace, I have to get into college." – NIEMA

Like all students with that goal, Niema had to stay on top of things, meeting every deadline on time and figuring out dozens of unfamiliar requirements. In the following pages, she and other students who made it to college give some pointers on the admissions process—so that, in Niema's words, you can "make people with power care what's going on with your life."

Start planning as early in high school as you can.

Starting in ninth grade, you make decisions that will affect your path to college. As you go about selecting your high school courses, signing up for extracurricular activities, getting support, and doing homework, you are developing the strengths that will show up on your college applications later.

But it's not all about waiting for a college to say yes to you. You decide where to apply, and the earlier you start considering what you want, the better your chances of getting it. As you find out more about what you like and don't like, you can start to compile a list of colleges that appeal to you.

》 I think you should start freshman year. Things are easier when you plan ahead of time: "Okay, what does it take for me to graduate from high school, what does it take for me to get into college?" In Oakland public schools, you need only two years of math. You could very well graduate from college and not have the required courses to get into college. So you have to figure that out. Then ask, "What are some possible colleges that I can get into?"

The earlier you start, the easier it is for you to be picky, to find something that you really like. You want to have a list of what it is you're looking for in a school, so you can rule some schools out. - NIEMA

You can reduce your stress in senior year if you take a look at some college applications well beforehand. Rosa discovered very late what a long time they required to fill out, and then she had to deal with panic as well as lots of paper.

》 I don't think I ever imagined what it took to do the application—if I had known, I would have done it way in advance. I did not know till my second semester of senior year, so I was very overwhelmed. There are many things you need to know—like that you have to pay for every application that you send. How would I know that? That's something very important. How should I write my college essay*? Where do I get help? I was in a rush because the deadline was coming, so I just did everything in two weeks.

In my particular school we did have a lot of help. However, students were mostly applying to state schools and community colleges, and that is fairly easy to do. But for a student who wants to do something else and has higher expectations for herself, the application process can be overwhelming. - ROSA

Make a "to-do" list and share it with your parent or guardian.

Even though your family has no experience with college admissions, it is usually a good idea to share your thinking and planning with your parent or guardian. (If you expect them to discourage you, you might ask your guidance counselor to join the conversation.) You can fill out your actual college applications on your own, but when you apply for financial aid,

---

* A personal essay you write about yourself, which is required on most college applications.

both you and your parents must provide information from income tax forms. These materials can take a long time to compile, so your family will need some advance warning.

Also, your family may also have strong feelings about whether you go away to school. Those conversations call for patience and communication on both sides, Niema found.

» There's always going to be this tension of "You don't understand." You're like, "Well, you didn't go, so you don't know!" When you start going through the stress, like "Who's going to accept me, where am I going to apply, how am I going to get this money," you have to realize that your parents are just as stressed about the situation as you are. Maybe they're not going through the exact same thing, but you are their child, and so they're going through the anxiety.

My mom wanted me to stay in California and be close to home, and I wanted to go off and explore, and be this adventurous person: "Oh, I'm going to go where there's nobody I know, I'm going to start my life all over again!" But when it came down to it, she was just like, "Well, you're going to college and that's what matters, so go ahead and handle that." – NIEMA

Not all parents let go of their children so easily. At the end of her senior year, Aileen got into her first-choice college, the John Jay College of Criminal Justice, in New York City. That summer, she began taking the bus from her home in New Jersey to an introductory writing class the college required.

» I really did like the school, I enjoyed everything about going there. But my parents really didn't like the idea, because of the simple fact that it was in New York. The class was from six to ten at night, so at three I just went straight from work, and I got home at twelve-thirty at night on the bus by myself. That really wasn't good, they worried that something would happen to me. They said, "You're not going back, pick another college." I was seventeen, so I had to do what they told me to. I didn't have time to pick another college, so I just went to the community college, where the only thing I had to do was register for the classes. – AILEEN

Aileen accepted her parents' decision, partly because she agreed that her commute was putting her at risk. However, many colleges have counselors who can help you with such practical issues, large or small. When Karen moved with her child to another town to go to college, for example, she could not get into the dorm apartment she had rented.

>> We were like staying here, staying there, and it was really getting to my son. So I went to the university housing office and said, "Can you help me get back into my apartment?" They made some phone calls, and sure enough, I got in the next day. - KAREN

Make connections with students who went to college before you.

Niema's leadership class teacher helped connect his students who went off to college with others who were still in high school, making their plans. Those connections can make a big difference as you decide where to apply, Niema says.

>> People who graduated from your high school have gone off to somewhere else, and most likely there is somebody still at your school that knows them. Maybe it's a vice principal, maybe it's a counselor—people don't just graduate and forget their high school ever existed! There's somebody there who has that connection that you can pick up on. That can get you where you need to be, or get you to talk to people who will put you on the right track. - NIEMA

Practice writing personal essays, before you need one for your application.

Many colleges will ask you to include a personal essay in your application, so they can get a better sense of who you are and how you think. As the first in your family to go to college, you have something important to tell them in this essay. Admissions boards will take a real interest in how you came to be the person you are. The challenges you have faced, the people who inspired you, the obstacles you have overcome, and your hopes for the future are all good topics for a college essay.

>> I wanted to identify an experience of my own to write about, and I had to really think about what I wanted the admissions person to know about me. I wanted to talk about my experiences as an immigrant—what it was for me to come from another country and completely immerse into a new culture and a new kind of education. Reading other people's personal narratives, in books and in class, really helped. In the end, I wrote about my grandmother, who raised me in my home country while my mother came to America to work. I revised that essay at least fifteen times, and I really enjoyed thinking about my own experience—what brought me to this country, and where I was headed. - ROSA

If you keep a journal in high school, you might draw on it for ideas to get you started when the time comes for the application essay. Writing poetry also can help free up your thoughts and emotions and give you new ideas that you can develop later in an essay. If your English teacher assigns the class to write a personal essay (or even a letter to the editor), consider it as a tryout for the application essay, and ask for feedback on how to make it better. And, like Rosa, go through as many drafts as you possibly can.

Make a plan for your college entrance tests.

Most colleges require some form of standardized tests before they accept you—but not all. Quite a number of selective colleges now ask only for your grades from high school courses and recommendations from your teachers.*

To make sure you have the most options, early in eleventh grade, start asking your guidance office about prep courses for both the SAT and the ACT. (Some colleges have policies about which of these tests they want you to take.) The more you get familiar with the tests, the better you will do on them. Schedules for giving those tests are set early, so it is worth putting them on your calendar.

Late in his senior year, when Eric decided to apply to Wake Forest University, he was alarmed to discover that they required SAT tests, for which he felt totally unprepared. It took some doing on the part of his mentor, but the college eventually agreed to convert his ACT score to an SAT equivalent.

---

*You can get a list of such colleges at www.fairtest.org/optinit.htm.

>> As I started getting everything together for the application, I realized that I hadn't in four years in high school been told to take an SAT. I had only been prepped for ACT. So when my mentor said, "You need to take the SAT two days from now!" I was like, "What? No prep!?" You know, the SAT is totally different from the ACT.

I was not registered in time. I had to pray that somebody would not show up for their test so I could take their place. Everybody showed up, but one girl said, "I am not taking this test," and she leaves. I'm like, "*I'll take her test!*" So I'm freaking out, and I'm in there, and everybody pulls out calculators. I had none of that. I took the test, but I did horribly! However, they turned my ACT score into an SAT score, and it was good enough to get in. So it was like, "Okay, you're good! Breathe!" - ERIC

Get help from all sides. It is not just you—the application process is complicated.

Don't let the paperwork discourage you from applying for college and financial aid. If you need someone to help you do it, ask—your guidance office, your mentor or employer, even a teacher. If no one can answer your question, you can also call the college itself. They are used to answering questions, especially about the financial aid application.

Eric got help from his internship supervisors, but in the end he had to sit down with his mother and go over the family's records.

>> Doing the financial aid forms, that whole process was hard. I didn't know what the heck I was doing—I would sit down at the computer and just cry! I would just look at the screen like, "What are you asking me? I don't know what this means! I don't have this! Mom, as busy as you are, sit down with me, help me." And dealing with a parent who does not know how to use a computer, that was the longest process of my life—like, "*Mom!* What are you doing!!"

My advice is just keep a record of what you're doing in the whole process. Have Social Security numbers handy, have bills handy, keep all your receipts, keep all your bank statements if you have them. Through the whole process, I put together a binder of everything I was supposed to have, copies and dates of stuff that I turned things in, student loans, promissory notes, all that stuff. I have copies of my Fafsa*, of CSS Profile*, of the application itself. Even for stuff that I had to do online I printed it out, and I have all of it. You're going to have to send multiple copies of multiple copies of the same thing!

The hardest thing was trying to pinpoint what our income was. And I know the financial aid committee was like, "You've got to be kidding, this kid has nothing, I mean nothing!" I never had to do something like that before, having to prove our living situation. And because it's already below the poverty level, trying to explain why when they say, "This doesn't match up, how are you able to survive off of just this?" – eric

Remember, once you are in college you must apply again for financial aid every year, in the early spring. As a high school senior, Niema got help from a volunteer at CollegeWorks, an organization that mentors students through the college and financial aid application process*. By the second time around, as a first-year college student, she felt more confident doing it herself.

» My mom was working, my step-dad was working, raising a family, they didn't have time to do all the paperwork for me, so senior year I worked with a program called CollegeWorks. They had a financial aid counselor who told me what forms I needed to get done, gave me the paperwork, the worksheets. Based on his advice, I filled out all my forms to get my aid for freshman year. Right now the time is coming up again for me to do financial aid, so I called my mom: "Send me your tax papers, so I can fill out all these forms, I'm handling this on my own." – niema

Look for scholarships intended for people like you.

Many students do not know about the huge number of scholarships, usually from private donors, that are reserved for students with particular backgrounds or interests. Some may go only to students from a particular minority group, and others to students who are the first in their family to attend college. There are scholarships just for choir singers, hockey

---

* Free Application for Federal Student Aid, a required financial aid application form administered by the U.S. Department of Education.

* College Scholarship Service Profile, a financial aid application form administered by the College Board and required by many colleges.

* See more about CollegeWorks at www.collegeworks.org.

players, people who like to volunteer, gay and lesbian students, disc jockeys, and just about any other category you can think of. Start early in your senior year to search for these scholarships using Internet services* that will send you emails as application deadlines approach.

Businesses also often sponsor scholarships for students in their area. Stephen tells in Chapter 3 about how various people he knew in the community wanted to help him to go to the University of Texas, located right there in town. Once he was accepted, local organizations showed their support with scholarship dollars.

》 We had scholarships available from the outside communities around Austin, around Texas, and national scholarships. The school set up a career counselor who would actually solicit donations from local organizations and businesses with connections to our high school community—Rotary Club, Hispanic Chamber of Commerce, my church. They had scholarships given out in those businesses' names, at our graduation and award assemblies. I got a great one from the electric company, the Lower Colorado River Authority, which controls water usage along the Colorado River.

If I used those connections to my best interest, by getting community scholarships from organizations that wanted to help out young Latinos, I knew I'd be able to supplement a lot of my need. So I filled out applications. When the electric company called me in for an interview, they sent me down to this big room and people just fired questions at me. I remember one was, "What's your hardest class?" They also asked me about athletics, and what I thought about current events in the news, like the ruling against prayer at football games, because I was heavily involved with the Fellowship of Christian Athletes. – STEPHEN

Starting early in your high school years, it helps to practice talking to adults about issues that you care about, so that you will feel at ease later, in interviews like the one Stephen describes. When the time comes for an interview, brainstorm with friends beforehand about questions you may expect. As you answer them, remember to talk specifically about your own experiences, challenges, and accomplishments in high school.

---

* For example, www.fastweb.com.

Your decisions about college will probably not be over when you hear back from colleges with their acceptances, rejections, or offers to put you on a waiting list. Each college decides on its own what financial aid package to offer, and you may have to balance how much you want to go to a place against how much it will cost.

Niema suggests contacting the college by letter or phone after you are accepted, if you want to present your case for an increase in their financial aid award.

» If they don't give you a financial aid package that you agree with, you can appeal. You can present a letter, "Here's why that financial aid package wasn't enough for me. I really want to go to your school, and obviously you think I'm good enough because you accepted me. So these are my conditions, I need this much money to go here! Yeah, it says we make this much money, but my mom had to take out a loan for whatever, or my dad hasn't been working for the past few months because of illness," or different things like that. There are some things that applications don't ask, but they honestly factor into what you can afford. (Niema)

If you are put on a waiting list for admission, it also helps to write one more letter to a college where you really want to go. In it, you should describe anything new that you have done since you first sent in your application. Tell the admissions officers again how much you want to attend that college, and why. Remind them that you will be the first in your family to go to college, and what a long and hopeful road you have traveled to this point. When the time comes to select students from the waiting list, that one last letter about yourself can only increase your chances.

Conclusion

You're on your way

*T*he wonderful and careful work ahead of you is just beginning, if you are the first in your family to go to college. You are the pilot on a long journey, taking off from an airport with your flight plan. At the start, you will communicate with people who have useful information to help you map your course. Once in the air, you will stay constantly alert, making new decisions and adjustments as the situation around you changes.

Like all good pilots, you should keep up a regular conversation with those who have made that same flight before you. Starting right now, you can find out who they are, then ask them to tell you how they did it. They really want to tell you more about their experiences, and you can use what they say to make your own journey easier.

In the last pages of this book, we offer some tools to help you through that process. Our next section lists resources to which you can turn for the information you need. We end the book with a planning checklist, reminding you of important actions to take during each year of high school.

In the end, your own desire and commitment will make the biggest difference to your success. Like the students in this book, you have the intelligence it takes to get to college, but it also takes hard work and persistence in your classes. At times, your progress may seem slow, and not everything you try will work out well. If you feel discouraged, you can start new conversations and make new connections with the people who inspire you—and you, in turn, will inspire them.

Have courage, and good luck!

Useful Resources

Staying organized and on time in your quest for college can sometimes feel like another part-time job—but don't quit! Just take it in small, steady steps. The following pages offer helpful resources, ending with a checklist you can use year by year, to plan your progress and keep track of important dates.

PREPARING FOR COLLEGE

College Board
www.collegeboard.com
In addition to providing all the information you need about the PSAT's and SAT's, the College Board website also has tools for planning for college, and finding and applying to college. It offers a useful interactive tool called "My Organizer" that is well worth signing up for.

ACT, Inc.: A Student Site for ACT Test Takers
www.actstudent.org
Includes information about registering for the ACT's, test prep, financial need estimator, and tips on college and career planning.

Prep for College Calendar
www.nacac.com
The National Association for College Admission Counseling explains what you can do in your high school freshman, sophomore, junior, and senior years to prepare for college.

Choosing the Right College
www.collegeispossible.org
A list of recommended Web sites, books and brochures from College Is Possible.

Preparing Your Child for College: A Resource Book for Parents
www.ed.gov/pubs/Prepare
This resource from the U.S. Department of Education provides information for parents on why their child should attend college, preparing for college, selecting a college, and financing a college education.

Black Excel

www.blackexcel.org

A comprehensive resource especially dedicated to African-American families and first-generation college students. The website includes detailed information about preparing for college, scholarships, historically black colleges (including virtual tours), and summer enrichment programs for high school minority students. There's also a free newsletter.

PAYING FOR COLLEGE

The Student Guide

www.studentaid.ed.gov

Available in English and Spanish, The Student Guide is a comprehensive resource on student financial aid from the U.S. Department of Education.

Financial Aid Resources

www.nacac.com

The National Association for College Admission Counseling provides this list of links to scholarships, lenders and other resources. Go to their "Online Resources" and then click on "financial aid."

A Brief Look at Student Financial Aid Programs

www.collegeispossible.org

The College is Possible website offers "Paying for College," an overview of federal grants and loans; tax benefits for college students; and other federal, state and institutional programs.

Multicultural Resources

www.nacac.com

A list of counseling and financial aid sources to assist students from various ethnic and cultural backgrounds, from the National Association for College Admission Counseling. Go to their "Online Resources" and then click on "Multicultural Resources."

FastWeb

www.fastweb.com

This free service from Monster.com allows users to search over 600,000 scholarships worth more than $1 billion.

Your Planning Checklists, Year by Year

Your journey to college starts early in high school, and so for each year, it helps to have a checklist of your progress. Take the section that matches your current grade level, and post it where you can look at it often (on your wall, or taped to the front of a notebook). At the end of each year, save that year's completed checklist in a special folder marked "College." It will help you keep on track and organized, and remind you of important information when the time comes to apply to college in your senior year.

GRADE 9

☐ Let your teachers know that you plan to go to college.

☐ Are your courses considered "college prep"? If you don't know, ask your guidance counselor to make sure they are.

> **TIP** Colleges like to see challenging courses on your record, even if you get lower grades in them.

> **TIP** If you want to play sports in college, you should know that college athletic teams have requirements about what high school courses you take.

☐ Let your teachers get to know you better. For a start, write down the names of the ones you trust or admire most:

1. _____

2. _____

3. _____

☐ Do you know other students like you who are planning to go to college? It helps to share your ideas and plans with them. Write down the names of the ones you trust or admire most:

1. _____

2. _____

3. _____

☐ Read as much as you can this year. It will give you new ideas, make you a better thinker, and build your vocabulary. Start a list of things you enjoy reading:

1. _____

2. _____

3. _____

4. _____

5. _____

☐ Get involved in activities you care about—at school and after school (including sports, clubs, community service, church group, jobs, etc.). List the ones that most appeal to you:

1. _____

2. _____

3. _____

☐ Think about your current interests. What career fields might match up with them? As you get new ideas, write them here:

YOUR INTEREST   CAREER FIELDS CONNECTED WITH IT

1. _____

2. _____

3. _____

☐ Start to look for information about colleges that fit with your interests. The guidance office will have books, catalogs, and posters, or you can check out colleges on the Internet. (Just type "college search" into Google or any search engine.) If you find any that appeal to you, write their names on this list, using extra space if you need it:

NAME OF COLLEGE   CAREER FIELDS CONNECTED WITH IT

1. _____

2. _____

3. _____

☐ Make a folder or large envelope marked "Grade 9 Portfolio" and save your best work in it, so it won't get lost. This should include class assignments, but don't forget to include poems, artwork, or evidence of other things you do outside of school.

☐ Use your summer to have fun while you learn. Ask your guidance office about enrichment programs (camps, summer courses) that help students like you prepare for college.

☐ Keep taking the most challenging courses you can.

☐ If you are having trouble with your schoolwork, ask for help. If the teacher doesn't have time for you, ask another adult or a student who is doing well in that class.

☐ Which teachers do you connect with best this year? Write their names here:

1. _____

2. _____

☐ Stay involved in the activities you most care about—at school, after school, and in the summer. Which ones do you most care about this year? List them here:

1. _____

2. _____

3. _____

TIP The more you care about your extra activities, the more they matter to college admissions. Don't do things just to make a longer list—better to do a few things well.

☐ Go to www.collegeboard.com and sign up for a free student account. Once you do this, go to "My Organizer" and it will help you get through your "to-do" list for tests and applications. Take it step by step—it's easier than it looks!

☐ Early in September, ask your guidance counselor to help you sign up for preliminary college admissions tests like the PSAT. Your scores on these will not count when you apply to college, and they are good practice for later.

TIP Many college entrance tests like these charge a fee. If you cannot afford the fee, ask your counselor to help you apply for a waiver, so you can take the test anyway.

TIP When you get your test results, ask your guidance counselor or a teacher to explain how to make sense of the scores. If you hope to do better next time, ask about what kind of extra preparation you will need.

☐ In April, ask your guidance counselor to help you register for the SAT Subject Tests, given in June. These one-hour exams test you on academic subjects such as biology, chemistry, math, physics, and foreign languages. Take SAT Subject Tests soon after you complete a course in that subject. (Select the "score choice" option. This way, you can take more Subject Tests in eleventh and twelfth grades, and then send colleges only your best results.)

TIP Many colleges require three SAT Subject Tests. Some colleges recommend or require Math Level 1 or Math Level 2. Not all SAT Subject Tests are given on every test date. Check the calendar carefully to determine when the Subject Tests you want are offered, and plan using "My Organizer" on www.collegeboard.com.

☐ Keep making notes about how your interests and passions might connect to college or careers later.

YOUR INTEREST   RELATED CAREER FIELDS   POSSIBLE COLLEGES

1. _____

2. _____

3. _____

☐ Ask your counselor about summer enrichment opportunities like Upward Bound. If you can't find one in your area, go to www.google.com and search for "youth college readiness summer programs." (Add the word "minority" if it applies to you.)

☐ Look at this list and check any other summer activities you could explore:

___ Volunteer at a workplace that interests you (like a library, a radio station, a YMCA)

___ Sign up for a career exploration course or program at a local community college

___ Participate in music, art, theatre, or dance offerings in your community

___ Take a course that will help you do better on college admissions tests

___ Practice computer skills at your public library

___ Write your own ideas here:

_____

_____

_____

☐ Get together with several classmates and talk about what you have been doing to explore your college plans.

☐ Keep reading as much as you can. Make a list of all the books you read this year. Put a star next to the ones you liked the best, and make a note as to why.

1. _____

2. _____

3. _____

4. _____

5. _____

☐ Make a folder or large envelope marked "Grade 10 Portfolio" and save your best work in it, so it won't get lost. This should include class assignments, but don't forget to include poems, artwork, or evidence of other things you do outside of school.

☐ At the start of the year, make a special folder marked "College." Keep everything connected to your college planning here—information, schedules, forms, and anything else.

☐ Check test schedules for PSAT, SAT or ACT, and register yourself for tests on "My Organizer" at www.collegeboard.com.

TIP Many college entrance tests like these charge a fee. If you cannot afford the fee, ask your counselor to help you apply for a waiver, so you can take the test anyway.

☐ Find out where "test prep" courses are given, and sign up for them.

TIP The more familiar you are with college admission tests, the better you will do on them. Take practice tests as often as you can.

☐ Attend a college fair to get more information about colleges. You can also write, telephone, or use the Internet to ask colleges to send you materials.

☐ Don't delay college planning because your family cannot afford to pay for college. Low-income students receive funding—from the government and sometimes the college—to help meet college costs.

☐ Colleges want to see demanding courses on your grade 11 schedule. Use this space to list the most challenging courses that you can take this year:

1. _____

2. _____

3. _____

4. _____

5. _____

☐ Junior year grades are very important in college admissions. If you are having trouble with your schoolwork, ask for help. If the teacher does not have time for you, ask another adult or a student who is doing well in that class.

☐ At the end of your junior year, you will need to ask two teachers to write you a letter of recommendation to go in your school file. Choose the teachers who know you the best (even if you didn't have them this year), and write their names here:

1. _____

2. _____

TIP Don't be shy about asking for a recommendation. Just say, "You were an important teacher for me, and I wonder if you would consider writing me a college recommendation and giving it to my guidance counselor." (Only the college and the guidance office, not you, are allowed to see the recommendation.)

☐ Stay involved in the activities you most care about—at school, after school, and in the summer. Which ones do you most care about this year? List them here, along with any leadership role you have in them:

1. _____

2. _____

3. _____

TIP Colleges also will look at recommendations from adults who know you through your job or other out-of-school activities. If you know someone like this, write his or her name here. Ask that person to send a letter to your guidance office, too.

1. _____

☐ Keep reading as much as you can. Make a list of all the books you read this year. Put a star next to the ones you liked the best, and make a note as to why.

1. _____

2. _____

3. _____

4. _____

5. _____

☐ Narrow down your list of colleges to six—two "safety schools" that you think will probably accept you, two "top choices," and two in between. If possible, talk over your choices with your parents at this point.

TOP CHOICES   IN BETWEEN   SAFETY

1. _____ 2. _____ 3. _____

1. _____ 2. _____ 3. _____

1. _____ 2. _____ 3. _____

☐ Look for summer opportunities that give you a taste of the college experience. One of the colleges on your list might have a program for high school students—call and ask! (Don't forget to tell them that you will be the first in your family to go to college.)

☐ Ask your school if they arrange a "college visit" trip for juniors and seniors. If they don't, plan your own with family or friends over the summer.

☐ Make a folder or large envelope marked "Grade 11 Portfolio" and save your best work in it, so it won't get lost. This should include class assignments, but don't forget to include poems, artwork, or evidence of other things you do outside of school.

☐ Your "College" folder will become quite large this year, so keep it organized! If you want, turn it into a file box, containing separate folders for testing documents and score reports, applications for admission, applications for financial aid or scholarships, copies of your income tax forms, notes for your application essay, completed planning checklists from grades 9 through 11, and so forth.

☐ Choose challenging courses this year, and work hard in them. Your performance senior year shows admissions people that you can go on to succeed in college.

☐ Register for the SAT Reasoning Test, SAT Subject Tests, or ACT tests given in the fall or early winter. Don't forget to ask for your scores to be sent to the colleges on your list.

☐ In fall of senior year, attend another college fair to gather information about colleges and talk to their representatives. If you find new ones that interest you, use the chart below to revise the list you made on your Grade 11 planning checklist:

TOP CHOICES	IN BETWEEN	SAFETY
1. _____	2. _____	3. _____
1. _____	2. _____	3. _____
1. _____	2. _____	3. _____

☐ Take every chance to actually visit the colleges that interest you. Call the admissions office and see if you can arrange an interview—colleges do not require them, but it can help your chance of getting in.

☐ Find out your Social Security number (and/or your green card number, if you are a legal immigrant), which you must have for your college applications. If you do not have a Social Security number, but you qualify for one, contact the closest Social Security office (www.ssa.gov) as soon as possible to obtain a number. Write your number here:

☐ Decide six colleges you are actually going to apply to. Write their names in the chart below, and check whether you will apply online, use the Common Application (www.commonapp.org), or send in a paper application. Then write the deadline for each college—not all colleges have the same deadline!

COLLEGE NAME	Apply online?	Mail in paper application?	Use common application?	Deadline
1. _____	☐	☐	☐	_____
2. _____	☐	☐	☐	_____
3. _____	☐	☐	☐	_____
4. _____	☐	☐	☐	_____
5. _____	☐	☐	☐	_____
6. _____	☐	☐	☐	_____

TIP Most colleges charge you an application fee, but some colleges waive that fee if you apply online using the Common Application. If you cannot afford the fee, ask your guidance counselor for a fee waiver, or call the college admissions office yourself and explain the situation.

☐ For each college on your list, make sure you complete all applications for financial aid. Every college requires the FAFSA (www.fafsa.ed.gov), and some colleges also require a form called CSS PROFILE (find it at www.collegeboard.com). Many colleges even have another form of their own to fill out. Use the chart below to keep everything straight, including the deadline for each different application.

COLLEGE NAME	FAFSA		CSS PROFILE		College fin. aid app	
	Deadline	Completed	Deadline	Completed	Deadline	Completed
1. _____	_____	☐	_____	☐	_____	☐
2. _____	_____	☐	_____	☐	_____	☐
3. _____	_____	☐	_____	☐	_____	☐
4. _____	_____	☐	_____	☐	_____	☐
5. _____	_____	☐	_____	☐	_____	☐
6. _____	_____	☐	_____	☐	_____	☐

TIP In January, you and your parents should file your income taxes, because you will need them in order to fill out the FAFSA and other financial aid forms. If your family does not file taxes because its income is too low, indicate that when you complete the FAFSA application. Then telephone each college's financial aid office to request a waiver form, which you can send them instead of your income tax forms.

TIP Financial aid applications always ask for your parent's signature. If your situation does not permit this for any reason, call the college financial aid office to explain, and they will tell you what to do.

☐ Apply for as many scholarships as you can find. (Use www.fastweb.com, and ask your guidance counselor for local scholarships from businesses or organizations.) On the chart below, write down the names and deadlines for the ones you qualify for, and keep track of deadlines:

ORGANIZATION THAT GIVES THE SCHOLARSHIP	DEADLINE	COMPLETED
_____	_____	☐
_____	_____	☐
_____	_____	☐
_____	_____	☐

☐ Meet with your guidance counselor to go over your grades and other information you will need to fill out the college applications. Ask your counselor to check if the teachers who said they would write recommendations have done it yet. (If not, go back and ask them again—they probably just forgot.)

TIP Write thank-you notes to those who write recommendations and keep them informed of your decisions.

☐ Get together with a friend who is also applying to college, and spend a day filling out application forms. If possible, meet in a place with access to a copy machine. Bring fine-tipped black pens, white-out to cover up any mistakes, and extra paper for making drafts and notes. Use your best printing when you fill out the forms. You should complete the "personal essay" section on another day—it is a project in itself. (See next page.)

TIP From your "College" folder, pull out the lists you made in grades 9, 10, and 11 about your activities, reading lists, etc. They will help you as you fill out your applications.

☐ Take a few hours to prepare for writing the personal essay you will need on your college applications. Think back on your whole life up to this point, and make a list of moments that you remember especially well. Whether they were happy or difficult times for you, write down notes about each of them here. (Use extra space if you need it.)

1. _____

2. _____

3. _____

4. _____

5. _____

☐ Take another hour or two to yourself, and pick just one moment from the list you made of life memories. Then write down everything about it—what it felt like, what it looked like and sounded like, who was there, what felt important about it. Write freely, not stopping to worry about grammar or form, as if you were writing in your private journal. Then save those pages. Later, they will help you write the actual essay.

☐ Set aside a day or two to write the personal essay for your applications. (You can use the same essay for most applications.) Using some of the free writing you did about your life memories, describe one important moment to you in essay form. Use as many concrete details as you can—the college really wants to see how you notice and think about things. After you have something written, show it to your English teacher, your mentor, or anyone else you trust, and ask for feedback. Then revise, revise, revise through many drafts.

TIP Some colleges ask for more than one essay. Usually one of them is more personal, and the other asks about your reading, your activities, or why you want to go to that college. For the second essay, look back at your list of memories, but also look through your Portfolios for grades 9, 10, and 11.

TIP Somewhere in one of your application essays, let the reader know that you will be the first in your family to go to college. If it doesn't fit anywhere else, put it at the end, connecting the experience you describe to your hopes for college.

☐ Once you start getting letters accepting you to college or putting you on a waiting list, you do not need to decide right away. Use this chart to compare the offers you receive:

COLLEGE NAME	Accepted or waitlisted?	Total costs for the year	Total financial aid offered (grants + loans)	Subtract your financial aid from the total costs, to get your actual costs for the year	College notified of your decision (by May 1)
1. _____	☐	_____	_____	_____	☐
2. _____	☐	_____	_____	_____	☐
3. _____	☐	_____	_____	_____	☐
4. _____	☐	_____	_____	_____	☐
5. _____	☐	_____	_____	_____	☐
6. _____	☐	_____	_____	_____	☐

TIP If your first-choice college puts you on its waiting list, write another letter to the admissions office, making clear that they are your first choice and that you would attend if they accept you. If you have any new activities or accomplishments since you sent in your application, describe them, too.

☐ By May 1, make your decision about what college you will go to, and let that college know. Also notify other colleges whose offers you are turning down.

Celebrate! You are going to be the first in your family to go on to college!

The student contributors

 John Berry graduated from high school in rural Indiana. After working for several years, he entered Indiana University– Purdue University Fort Wayne, in Fort Wayne, Indiana. He hopes to go on to graduate school and become a history professor.

 Jackie Comminello began college at the University of Colorado at Denver, where she studied for two years. Then she transferred to the adjacent Community College of Denver, to prepare for a career in dentistry.

 Joshua Cryer majors in electrical engineering technology and Spanish at Indiana University–Purdue University Fort Wayne. He has an ongoing engineering internship at the Fort Wayne center of International Truck and Engine Corp, and also takes part in many campus activities.

 Rosa Fernández learned English in her New York City high school after arriving from the Dominican Republic at fourteen. She studies history at Wellesley College in Wellesley, Massachusetts, and intends to go on for her doctorate.

 Hazel Janssen left her Denver high school before graduating. After two years in the labor market, she returned to Emily Griffith Opportunity High School, through which she also takes community college courses at Denver Community College. She hopes for a career in the arts.

 Niema Jordan graduated from Oakland Technical Arts High School in California. A student at Northwestern University in Evanston, Illinois, she plans a double major in journalism and African-American Studies, and is running for campus office.

Naixing Lei arrived from China at sixteen in San Francisco, where he began learning English in high school. Now at City College of San Francisco, he plans to transfer to a four-year college and to prepare for a career in business.

 Mike Morris grew up in rural Mississippi, where he played football in high school. After studying for two years at a local community college, he transferred to Brigham Young University in Salt Lake City, Utah. He will major in recreational management and hopes to go on to earn a masters degree.

 Eric Polk went to high school in Nashville, Tennessee, where he worked as a youth leader at Community Impact, a nonprofit neighborhood organization. A student at Wake Forest University in Winston-Salem, North Carolina, he belongs to a men's singing group and teaches hip-hop to other students.

 Karen Powless combines her college studies in Grief and Victim Survivor Services with the responsibilities of marriage and children. She brings her young son with her to Oklahoma State University in Oklahoma City, where she is a leader in the Native American Students Association.

 Aileen Rosario finished high school in Paterson, New Jersey and works part time at the Paterson Education Fund. After two years at Passaic County Community College, she is going on to nearby Montclair State University. She hopes for a career in law.

 Stephanie Serda was raised outside Toledo, Ohio, and after graduating from high school she enrolled at Bowling Green State University. There she studies sport management, works at a local YMCA, and is active with the College Democrats.

 Stephen Torres grew up and graduated from high school in a rural area outside Austin, Texas. Now he studies at the University of Texas in Austin, Texas where he is active in the Latino Leadership Council.

Lumina Foundation for Education, a private, independent foundation, strives to help people achieve their potential by expanding access and success in education beyond high school. The Foundation bases its mission on the belief that postsecondary education remains one of the most beneficial investments that individuals can make in themselves and that society can make in its people.

> Lumina Foundation for Education
> 30 South Meridian Street, Suite 700
> Indianapolis, IN 46204
> www.luminafoundation.org

What Kids Can Do, Inc. (WKCD) is a national not-for-profit organization founded in 2001 for the purpose of making public the voices and views of adolescents. On its website, WKCD documents young people's lives, learning, and work, and their partnerships with adults both in and out of school. WKCD also collaborates with students around the country on books, curricula, and research to expand current views of what constitutes challenging learning and achievement.

> What Kids Can Do, Inc.
> P.O. Box 603252
> Providence, RI 02906
> www.whatkidscando.org

Next Generation Press is the book publishing arm of What Kids Can Do, Inc. With a particular focus on youth without privilege, we raise awareness of young people as a powerful force for social justice.

> Next Generation Press
> P.O. Box 603252
> Providence, RI 02906
> www.nextgenerationpress.org